Eco Alert!
ENERGY SUPPLY

Rebecca Hunter

FRANKLIN WATTS
LONDON•SYDNEY

First published in 2010 by
Franklin Watts
338 Euston Road
London NW1 3BH

Franklin Watts Australia
Level 17/207 Kent Street
Sydney NSW 2000

ISBN 978 0 7496 9321 3

Dewey classification number: 333.7'9

A CIP catalogue record for this publication
is available from the British Library.

Planning and production by
Discovery Books Limited
Managing Editor: Rachel Tisdale
Editor: Rebecca Hunter
Designer: Blink Media
Picture research: Colleen Ruck

Printed in China

Franklin Watts is a division
of Hachette Children's Books,
an Hachette UK Company.
www.hachette.co.uk

Photographs: **Alamy:** page 13 (Philip Wolmuth);
BioRegional: page 26; **Getty Images:** Cover
(Robin MacDougall/Photographer's Choice), page 7
(Marcel Mochet), page 15 top (Tim
Matsui/Liasion), page 21 (Issouf Sanogo), page 22
(Kim Steele), page 24 (Renaud Visage), page 28
(Larry W Smith); **Istock:** page 9 (Egdigital),
page 10 (Julia Nelson); **Newcast:** page 20 (Eon,
UK); **Shutterstock:** page 4 (Daniel Zuckerkandel),
page 5 (Bestweb), page 17 (Rodion), title page and
page 18 (Daniel Schoenen), page 19 (George
Bailey), page 25 (RCP Photo); **Wikimedia:** page
14/15 bottom (Martin St Amant).

Every attempt has been made to clear copyright.
Should there be any inadvertent omission please
apply to the publisher for rectification.

Contents

Blackout!

Can you imagine what would happen if our energy supply failed? If suddenly nothing worked? If the television you were watching, or the computer on which you were working, went dead? If the lights didn't come on in the evening, and the heating didn't work? If in a few days, all the food in the refrigerator and freezer was spoiled and there was no fuel to run the car? You would be cold, hungry and pretty unhappy.

This is not a plot for a science fiction movie. A **blackout** is a real possibility if we run out of energy.

Most of our energy supply comes from burning fuels such as coal, oil or natural gas. These fuels are called **fossil fuels** because they formed in the ground millions of years ago. Fossil fuels can be burned to give us heat. They can also be used to **generate** power in the form of electricity.

⊙ If we run out of power, we may have to read and work by candlelight again!

4

Most power stations like this one currently burn fossil fuels. These are non-renewable and will one day run out.

The world demand for energy is increasing. As the number of people in the world grows, more energy will be needed to run our homes, power our factories and drive our cars.

Relying on energy from fossil fuels has two main problems. Burning fossil fuels releases carbon dioxide and other **greenhouse gases** into the environment. These are contributing to **global warming**, an increase in temperatures around the world. Fossil fuels are also **non-renewable**. This means that once we have used them all there will be none left. The world is using so much energy that our fossil fuels supply will probably be used up in less than 200 years.

We need to find other, new sources of energy. We need to find them quickly, before our present supplies run out.

Energy for electricity

Electricity is a type of energy that we use to power many of our machines. It is generated in power stations. Most power stations burn the fossil fuels coal or oil.

The heat from burning the fuel is used to boil water. The steam from the boiling water turns **turbines** which then turn **generators**. The generators convert this movement into electricity. Electricity is transmitted by power lines, to homes, schools, offices and factories all over the country.

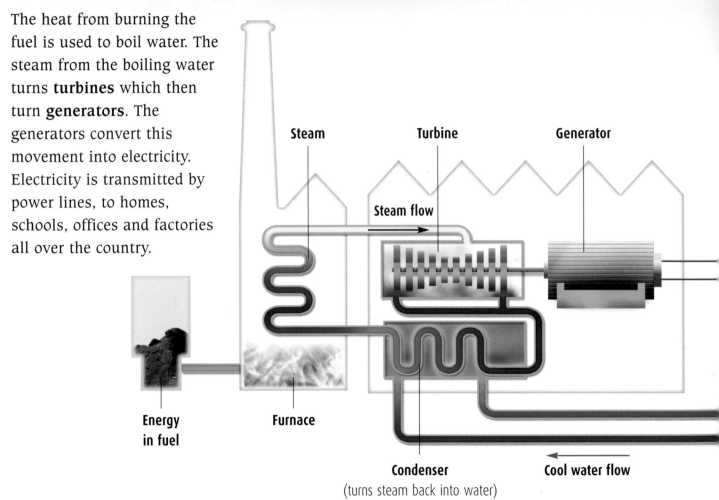

Steam

Turbine

Generator

Steam flow

Energy in fuel

Furnace

Condenser
(turns steam back into water)

Cool water flow

⊙ This diagram shows how electricity is generated in a fossil fuel-burning power plant.

Fossil fuel problems

When they are burned, fossil fuels create air **pollution**. All fossil fuels contain **carbon**. When they are burned, they give off the gas carbon dioxide (CO_2). Carbon dioxide is a greenhouse gas. Scientists believe that greenhouse gases are making the world warmer and changing the weather all over the planet.

All fossil fuels are found underground and extracting them is often very destructive to the environment.

Renewable energy

We need to make more use of forms of energy that are **renewable**. Renewable energy can be used again and again, and will never run out. We can get renewable energy in many ways: from the Sun, wind, water, living things and from beneath the ground.

At present only 18 per cent of the world's energy comes from renewable resources. To save the planet, this amount will have to increase in the future.

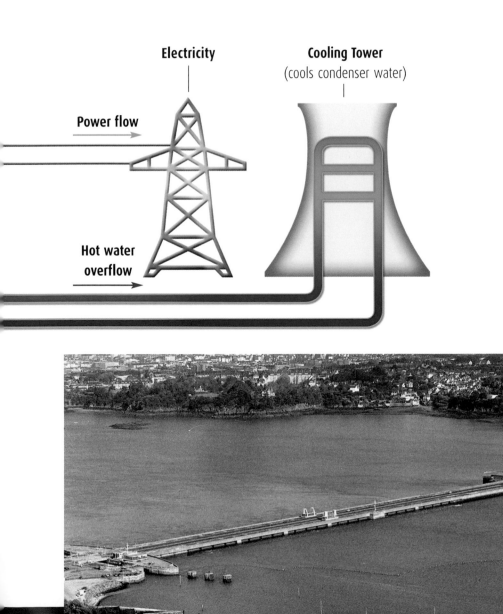

Electricity

Cooling Tower
(cools condenser water)

Power flow

Hot water overflow

HOTSPOT:

Tidal power

Tidal power is a form of renewable energy. The tides work twice a day every day of the year. This produces a large amount of energy that can be harnessed. At present there is only one large tidal power plant. It is at La Rance in France. It has been in operation for over 40 years and produces enough electricity to provide power for 20,000 homes.

Transport

As well as needing energy to generate electricity, we also need it to power our transport. Today people travel further and more often than they ever have before. They take buses to school, trains to work and go on holiday using ships and planes, as well as doing many kilometres in their cars.

Nearly all these vehicles burn different forms of oil, such as petrol or diesel, which pollutes the atmosphere. In **developed** countries, transport accounts for over 80 per cent of CO_2 emissions.

Saving fuel

If people used public transport more and their cars less, they could save fuel and reduce pollution. More governments need to make public transport cheaper and more reliable to encourage this.

Car manufacturers are now making smaller, lighter cars that are more fuel-**efficient**. Many people are swapping their big cars for these smaller models that travel much further on a tank of fuel.

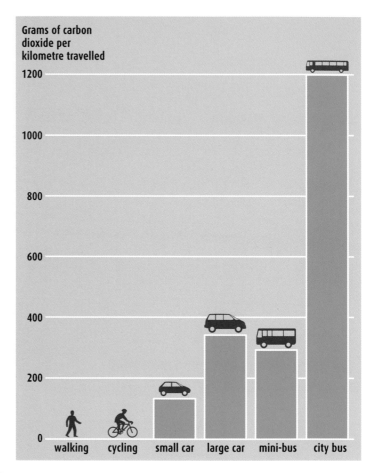

Grams of carbon dioxide per kilometre travelled

walking · cycling · small car · large car · mini-bus · city bus

⊙ This bar chart shows how much CO_2 various forms of transport make. A bus is the most polluting, but a bus can carry lots of people, so the amount of CO_2 created per person is much less than if one or two people were in a car.

Replacing oil

We need to find alternative ways of fuelling vehicles, not just to stop pollution but because the oil that produces the fuel is running out. About 60 per cent of the oil produced in the world is used for transport. At our present rate of use the world's known reserves of oil will run out by 2030.

How can you help?

Ten per cent of CO_2 in the atmosphere comes from aeroplanes. Encourage your parents to fly less often; you could use the train to go on holiday.

◉ Cars consume huge quantities of petrol and diesel and their exhaust gases are a major source of pollution.

Alternative energy sources

Scientists and engineers are working hard to find alternative energy sources for powering cars. Some cars are being designed to run on electricity and some on **solar power**. Fuels can also be made from **biomass**. Ethanol is the most widely used biomass fuel and can be made from various plants that contain **starch**. Unfortunately these plants take up room in fields once used to grow food (see page 21), but in the USA scientists are looking at ways of generating biomass energy from algae. Algae can be grown in both fresh and salt water and produce five times as much biomass per hectare as plants grown on land.

HOTSPOT:
Fuel cell vehicles

It is expected that within the next few years, fuel cell vehicles (FCVs) will be available for motorists. FCVs are powered by electric motors that generate their electricity using hydrogen fuel and oxygen from the air. These cars will be cheap to run and pollution-free; their only waste product will be water!

Energy from coal

Coal has been used as an energy resource for thousands of years. It is one of the easiest fossil fuels to extract and can therefore generate very large amounts of electricity quite cheaply.

Coal mining

Mining coal is a dangerous and messy business. Nearly half of all coal mined comes from surface mining. This is when huge machines dig for coal in open pits called **open-cast mines**. Surface mining destroys vegetation and wildlife and mines can cover areas of many square kilometres.

⊙ Open cast coal mining damages large areas of land. This former mine has been abandoned, leaving behind a landscape that is no use for agriculture, settlement or wildlife.

Pollution

Burning coal is a leading cause of **smog**, global warming and **acid rain**. In one year a typical coal-fired power station generates over 3 million tonnes of CO_2. Scientists are working on ways to prevent this pollution by capturing the CO_2 before it is released into the atmosphere and then storing it underground. This method, called carbon capture and storage (CCS), sounds like a good idea but it is expensive and has not yet proved practical.

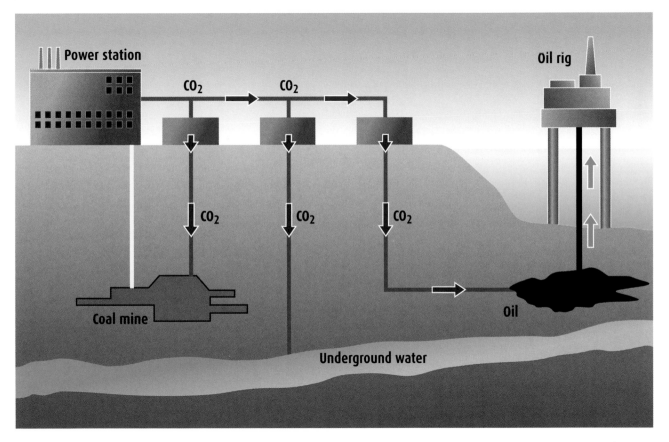

Importance of coal

Coal is mined in over 50 countries and the worldwide industry employs about seven million people. Many countries rely on their exports of coal for their national income. Although we need to reduce our dependence on coal as an energy resource, it will not be easy to remove it totally from world use.

⊙ In carbon capture and storage, CO_2 from burning coal is pumped into the ground to be stored. It can be stored in old coal mines, in underground water reserves or in the rocks from which oil has been extracted.

Oil and gas

Oil and natural gas are also found underground. Many reserves of oil and gas are under the sea and have to be drilled from offshore **rigs**. Once found, the oil or gas has to be transported to **refineries** by tankers or pipes.

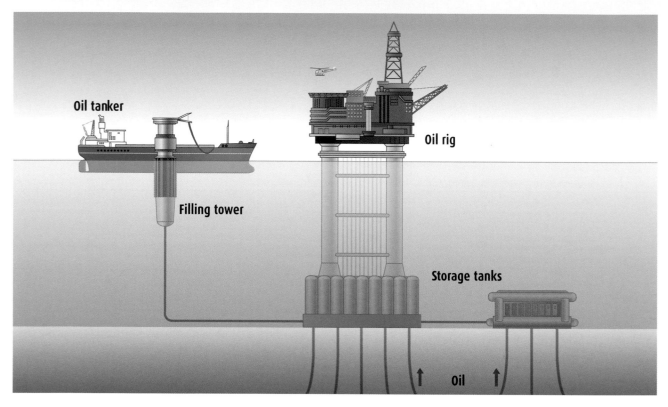

Oil tanker

Oil rig

Filling tower

Storage tanks

Oil

Environmental risks

One of the biggest problems with oil and gas extraction is the risk of leaks. When oil is accidentally spilled from pipes or tankers, it creates a thick black **slick** on the surface of the sea. This can be devastating to sea life for many years. In 1989 the *Exxon Valdez* oil tanker ran onto rocks in Alaska spilling 40 million litres of **crude oil** into the sea. Hundreds of thousands of birds and animals including sea otters, seals and orcas were killed. Over 20 years later the effects of the pollution have not fully disappeared and the damaged **ecosystem** is still struggling to recover.

◉ Oil is extracted from under the sea using offshore oil rigs, pipes and tankers. It is held in storage tanks underwater, until oil tankers take it away to be cleaned and processed at refineries.

⬆ The Druzhba oil pipeline is the longest in the world. It carries oil from south-east Russia to points in Ukraine, Hungary, Poland and Germany.

Oil and gas supplies

Much of the oil and gas sold today comes from Russia and countries in the Middle East. We need to buy oil and gas from them but their relationship with western countries is not always friendly and trading with them is often not easy.

Alternative sources

Fossil fuels provide about 86 per cent of the world's electricity today and are responsible for more than 90 per cent of greenhouse gas emissions. Finding alternative non-polluting energy sources is an important requirement for all the countries in the world.

HOTSPOT:

Amazon pipeline

Environmentalists are worried about plans to build the world's largest natural gas pipeline through 8,000km of South American wilderness. The pipeline will pass through the Amazon rainforest, with the loss of millions of trees and endangering local tribes and wildlife.

Hydroelectric power

One of the most widely used sources of renewable energy comes from hydroelectric power (HEP) – energy from water. Water always flows from high places to low places. HEP stations use turbines and generators to turn the energy in moving water into electrical energy. HEP is a very useful source of energy in countries with high mountains and high rainfall.

Environmental problems

Although HEP can create large amounts of clean energy, it does create some major environmental problems. When the dams are built, whole valleys are flooded and all the animals and people that live there lose their homes. When the Kariba HEP dam was built between Zambia and Zimbabwe in the 1950s, thousands of animals were rescued by *Operation Noah*, and over 50,000 local people were forced to leave their homes and farms.

Once a dam is built, the surrounding areas may be altered. Farm land can suffer from lack of fertile **silt** brought down by the river, or from droughts. Animal ecosystems that depended on the natural flow of the river may be destroyed.

A fish ladder is a series of pools that are built to allow salmon and other migrating fish to swim up the river to reach their spawning grounds. This picture shows the fish ladder on Bonneville dam which spans the Columbia River in Oregon, USA. Fish use this ladder to migrate upstream, bypassing the 60m high dam.

Fish, such as salmon and trout, that swim upstream to breed, are often prevented from reaching their breeding grounds by HEP dams.

Itaipu power station

The Itaipu power station on the Brazilian-Paraguayan border, is the largest HEP station in the world. The dam is over 7km long and took 13 years to build. It supplies Paraguay with 94 per cent of its electricity and Brazil with 20 per cent.

⊙ The Itaipu hydroelectric power plant is the largest development of its kind in operation in the world. Its construction used 12.3 million cubic metres of concrete and enough iron and steel to build 380 Eiffel Towers!

Wind power

People have used the power of the wind as an energy resource for hundreds of years to grind corn in windmills. Today wind energy can be harnessed to generate electricity.

Wind turbines

A modern wind turbine consists of a tower about 50m high with two or three blades which are attached to a generator. It is expensive to build wind turbines, but once they are up they have low running costs and last for about 25 years. The benefits of wind energy are that it needs no fuel, creates no pollution and will be available for ever. But it also has many downsides.

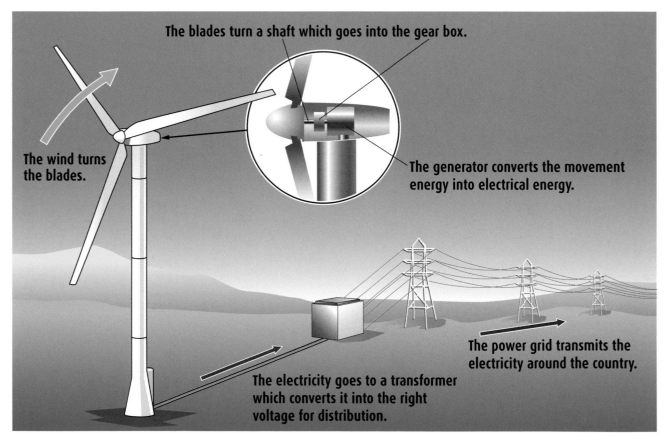

The blades turn a shaft which goes into the gear box.

The wind turns the blades.

The generator converts the movement energy into electrical energy.

The electricity goes to a transformer which converts it into the right voltage for distribution.

The power grid transmits the electricity around the country.

⊙ This diagram shows how electricity can be generated from the power of the wind.

Problems with wind power

A large amount of land is needed to build a wind farm. A big wind farm may cover an area of hundreds of square kilometres. Coastal areas and hills are often suitable places, but many people don't like the turbines spoiling the view of the countryside or the noise they make.

Wind turbines will only work on windy days, but if the wind is too strong they have to be shut down. At the moment they are not a very reliable source of power.

Offshore wind farms

Offshore wind farms are more expensive to build but raise fewer objections from people. The USA plans to build its largest offshore wind farm off the coast of Texas. Over 100 turbines will be erected about 8km offshore providing power for about 125,000 homes.

A danger to birds?

Many people are concerned that wind turbines may injure and kill birds. However radar studies show that birds usually pass by the turbines at a safe distance. Some birds may be killed, but power lines, masts and poles on land are much greater dangers to birds than wind turbines.

⊙ Offshore wind farms, like this one near Copenhagen, Denmark, receive steady winds, but they may be battered by waves and high winds.

Solar power

Using the Sun's energy to convert heat into electricity has huge **potential**. Every day the Sun generates more energy than the Earth's 6 billion people use in 30 years!

Using solar energy

The Sun's energy can be used to heat water or it can be converted directly into electricity using **photovoltaic** (pv) cells. You will have seen pv cells on calculators and some traffic signals. Some people cover the roofs of their houses with pv cells to provide some, or all of their domestic electricity.

⊙ Houses with solar panels can use the Sun's energy to heat their water and to make electricity.

⊙ This image shows photovoltaic cells in the desert. If just 4 per cent of the world's desert area was covered with pv panels, they could supply all of the world's electricity!

The power of the Sun can also be captured using giant lenses or mirrors to focus the sunlight. This method is called concentrating solar power (CSP) and is used by big solar thermal power plants.

Solar problems

Solar power plants need large areas of land. The Waldpolenz solar park in Germany will be the world's largest photovoltaic power system, covering 220 hectares of land. Solar power is an **intermittent** energy source – solar power is not available at night or on cloudy days, and so another energy source is needed to supplement it.

HOTSPOT:

Solar power in Spain

Europe's first commercial CSP power plant was built near Seville in southern Spain. Each solar power tower has 624 large, moveable mirrors called heliostats. The mirrors concentrate the Sun's rays onto the top of a tower where a solar receiver and a steam turbine are located. The turbine drives a generator producing electricity.

Biomass energy

Biomass energy comes from the energy trapped in living things such as plants and animal waste. This energy can be used as fuel. Many things can be used as biomass fuel, although the most common is wood from trees.

The Steven's Croft Biomass power station in Lockerbie, Scotland is the UK's largest wood-fired biomass station and supports a large forestry industry in the area. Here, the wood can be seen stacked up waiting to be burnt.

Biomass power stations

Biomass power stations run on different types of fuel. Some use trees or crops, such as bamboo or willow, that have been grown for use as biofuels. But many unwanted end products from agriculture and industry can also be used as biomass fuels. These could be wood from timber yards, waste left over after crops have been processed or even manure from livestock. The biomass can either be burned by itself in a power station – this method is called direct-firing, or it can be mixed with coal before burning.

Methane production

When biomass materials decompose they give off the gas **methane**. This is much worse for the environment than CO_2. However, biomass waste can be collected and fed into machines called **biodigesters**. As the solid waste breaks down and ferments, the methane gas is collected and stored in tanks. Later the methane can be burned to produce heat and power. The solid waste is made into fertilizer and sold to farmers. Some towns are beginning to collect household food waste and recycle it in this way.

Biomass problems

One of the drawbacks of biomass power is that it is expensive to collect, transport and store. Many people also think that using the land to grow crops for food is more important than growing crops for biomass.

◄ In Indonesia, precious rainforests are being cut down to plant palm oil plantations threatening many species of plants and animals. Palm oil is used in many food products worldwide and is increasingly used as a biofuel.

Geothermal energy

Deep below the Earth's surface the rock is under enormous pressure and is very hot. This heat energy can heat the water in the rocks underground to boiling point. This is called **geothermal** energy and we can use it to generate electricity. Geothermal energy is widely used in Iceland, New Zealand, Japan and the west coast of America.

Geothermal power stations

Geothermal power stations pipe the boiling water below the ground up to the surface. The steam from the water turns the turbines of the generators and produces electricity. Cooled water from the power station is pumped back into the ground to be heated up again.

⊙ This is the Geysers geothermal power plant in northern California, USA. The Geysers is the largest geothermal development in the world. It produces enough electricity to power 725,000 homes.

▶ In areas where underground rocks are very hot, the water in and around them is super-heated. The boiling water can be piped to the surface where the steam is used to turn turbines and generate electricity. Cooled water is pumped back down into the ground to be reheated and recycled.

Hot water on tap

In some areas the hot water can be pumped directly into towns and used directly to heat radiators, warm greenhouses and even to **pasteurise** milk!

Reliable energy

Geothermal energy may be one of the most reliable renewable energy methods available. It does not use up much land and once the power station is set up, it is fairly simple to keep running and the electricity generated is almost free. Geothermal energy requires no fuel and has no waste products.

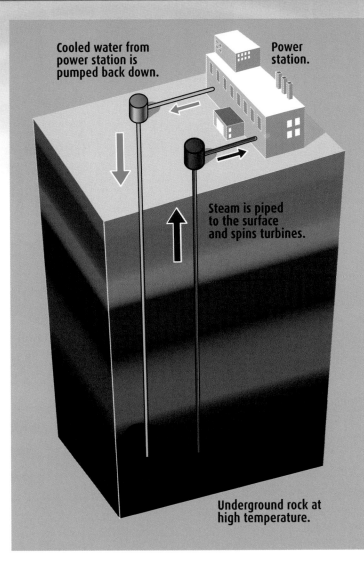

Cooled water from power station is pumped back down.

Power station.

Steam is piped to the surface and spins turbines.

Underground rock at high temperature.

Problems with geothermal energy

The main problem is that geothermal power stations can only be built in areas where hot rocks are close to the surface. Some people object to it because the release of steam from the power plants can be noisy and low levels of CO_2 are also given off.

One of the less well-known disadvantages of geothermal energy is that it can cause earthquakes in the surrounding areas. People who live in these areas suffer more earthquakes once water extraction has started. The earthquakes are not very strong but can damage the foundations of homes and other buildings.

How can you help?

How green is your energy supply? You can find out how electricity companies are involved in green energy on the Internet. Ask your school and your parents to sign up to a green home energy supplier.

Nuclear power

Nuclear power accounts for less than 20 per cent of the world's electricity. Many people think it is a good source of energy and that more nuclear power stations should be built. Others think it is a very dangerous way of generating electricity.

Nuclear fission

Nuclear energy is obtained from the splitting, or **fission**, of **atoms** in a fuel such as **uranium**. This splitting causes a nuclear reaction, and a tiny amount of **matter** changes into an enormous amount of heat energy. This heat is used in the same way as other power stations to boil water, turn generators and generate electricity.

Not renewable

Nuclear power cannot be classed as a renewable form of energy because it uses fuels, such as uranium. Much of the world's uranium comes from mines in Australia, Canada, South Africa and Kazakhstan. At our present rate of use, there are enough known sources of uranium to last 230 years.

HOTSPOT:

Nuclear power in France

France is the world leader in nuclear power. It has 59 nuclear power plants (like this one at Belleville-sur-Loire), which produce about 80 per cent of the country's electricity. France is the world's largest exporter of electric power and its electricity cost is among the lowest in Europe.

Nuclear waste

The nuclear reaction produces dangerous radioactive waste that must be disposed of very carefully. Some radioactive waste is buried underground in sealed containers, but people worry it will leak out or be released by earthquakes. Despite the fears about nuclear energy, many countries are finding it one of the best ways to supply their energy needs.

Remote power

Nuclear power is particularly useful for vessels which need to be at sea for long periods of time without refuelling. More than 150 nuclear-powered naval vessels have been built. Most are submarines but there are also icebreakers and aircraft carriers.

⊙ Many submarines, such as this Russian foxtrot class attack submarine, are nuclear powered. This means they can spend a long time underwater without having to come back to port to refuel.

Energy efficiency

As well as looking at new ways to get energy, we should see how efficiently we are using energy today. Most households and businesses could improve their energy efficiency.

Energy efficiency means using less energy to provide the same level of energy service. This is usually achieved by using more efficient products. For example, if you **insulate** your home and have double-glazed windows fitted, you will use less heat from your central heating to maintain the same temperature inside.

Energy-efficient appliances

You can now buy energy-efficient appliances, such as refrigerators, dishwashers, washing machines and dryers that use much less energy than older models. A new refrigerator bought today uses 40 per cent less energy than one bought in 2001.

⊙ The Beddington-Zero Energy Development in London has been designed so that it does not need outside energy for heating, lighting or power. The buildings are super-insulated and get their power for electricity from solar panels. The brightly-coloured chimneys remove warm, stale air, and heat up cool, clean air coming in.

Long life lightbulbs

Energy-saving, **fluorescent** lightbulbs give out the same amount of light as old **incandescent** lights but use less power and have a longer life. They will save 2,000 times their own weight in greenhouse gases, but they do contain the poisonous substance mercury which means they have to be disposed of carefully.

Standby savings?

Many machines such as televisions, DVD players and computers have a 'standby' mode which is supposed to save energy when you are not using the machine. Actually these standbys are wasting a lot of energy. It is estimated that in the USA $5 billion is spent each year on standby power. Some manufacturers are planning to remove standby buttons from machines in the future.

How can you help?

▶ Turn off the lights when you leave a room.

▶ Ask your parents to turn down your central heating. Just a change in 1°C (1.8°F) will cut your heating bill by up to 10 per cent.

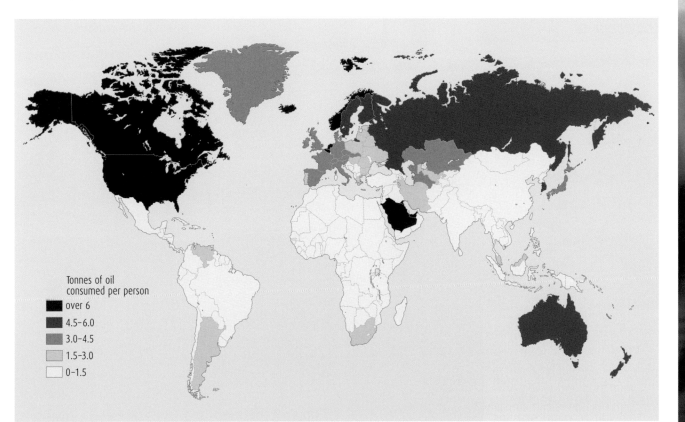

Tonnes of oil consumed per person

- ■ over 6
- ■ 4.5–6.0
- ■ 3.0–4.5
- ▨ 1.5–3.0
- ☐ 0–1.5

⊙ This map shows the energy consumption across the world. It has been measured as the equivalent of tonnes of oil used per person per year.

Future of energy

As the number of people in the world increases, their demand for energy is also going to increase. Many people in **developing countries** do not yet own the gadgets, machines and cars that we take for granted. In the next 20 years, the world's energy demand is expected to increase by up to 44 per cent.

The future for fossil fuels

We will continue to use fossil fuels for many years to come. This is because there is nothing yet as cheap, efficient and widely available as coal, oil and gas. They are a valuable source of energy, but if they are to be used in the future, better ways will have to be found to reduce the pollution they cause.

⊙ Many companies are changing the way they heat and light their buildings to reduce their energy bills and help save the environment. The Boeing aircraft company upgraded its lighting and reduced its electricity use by 90 per cent.

New energy sources

We need to find other ways of providing more energy. They need to be cheap, safe, renewable and environmentally friendly. Solar power is likely to become a more widespread choice. Many areas of desert could be covered with solar panels. Scientists are also looking at the possibility of putting satellites in space that would capture the flow of continuous energy from the Sun.

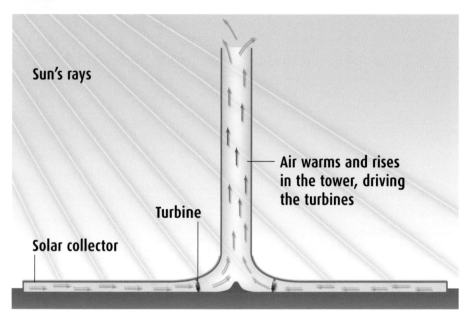

Sun's rays

Air warms and rises in the tower, driving the turbines

Turbine

Solar collector

◀ Some countries are looking at building solar towers. These would be nearly one kilometre high and would be surrounded with greenhouse-like solar collectors. Heat from the Sun would heat air in the collectors which would rise up the tower, turning turbines at the base of the tower.

Nuclear fusion

Nuclear fission is an important source of energy. However, it is unpopular with many people because of the dangerous radioactive waste products it leaves behind. Scientists are now looking for ways to make energy from a process called **nuclear fusion**, where atoms are fused together. This is extremely difficult to achieve, but if it were possible it would produce an unlimited supply of energy with much less dangerous waste than nuclear fission.

If our planet's future energy needs are to be met we need to act more responsibly today. For a sustainable future we must try and use less energy, waste less energy and make sure we obtain it from clean, renewable sources.

How can you help?

Save energy by:

▶ Keeping your heating and cooling appliances clean. Energy is lost when heating units have to work harder to draw air through dirty filters.

▶ Allowing your dishes to air dry: don't use the drying cycle in your dishwasher. This can save 20 per cent of your dishwasher's total electricity use.

▶ Selecting the most energy-efficient models when you replace your old appliances.

Glossary

Acid rain
Rain that has been made acidic by polluting gases in the atmosphere.

Atom
One of the tiny particles from which all materials are made.

Biodigester
A machine that can process plant and animal waste to create electricity.

Biomass
Organic matter such as plant material and animal wastes that can be used as fuel.

Blackout
When electrical power is cut off as a result of a shortage of energy.

Carbon
A chemical element that occurs in all living things.

Crude oil
Pure oil that is obtained from under the ground.

Developing country
Poorer countries where people have a low standard of living and low levels of industry.

Ecosystem
A community of living things together with their environment.

Efficient
Working well and preventing waste.

Environmentalist
A person who cares greatly about the environment.

Fission
The action of splitting something into two or more parts.

Fluorescent
Very bright and dazzling in colour.

Fossil fuels
Fuels including coal, oil and natural gas that were formed underground millions of years ago.

Generate
To produce something through a physical process.

Generators
Machines that turn moving energy into electrical energy.

Geothermal
Heat that comes from hot rocks beneath the Earth's surface.

Global warming
A rise in the average temperature of the Earth which many people think is caused by an increase of greenhouse gases in the atmosphere.

Greenhouse gas
Gases in the atmosphere such as carbon dioxide or water vapour that absorb heat that would otherwise escape into space.

Incandescent
Emitting visible light as a result of being heated.

Insulate
Something that prevents the passage of heat or electricity.

Intermittent
Something that happens from time to time.

Matter
The material that everything in the universe is made of.

Methane
A greenhouse gas.

Migrate
To move to a new habitat in response to seasonal changes or food supply.

Non-renewable
Something that will one day run out.

Nuclear fusion
The process of combining atoms to release energy.

Open-cast mines
Mines where coal is extracted from near the surface of the ground.

Pasteurise
To heat a liquid such as milk to a high temperature to destroy any bacteria in it.

Photovoltaic
Being able to generate electricity when exposed to sunlight.

Pollution
The act of making the environment dirty.

Potential
The possibility of something happening in the future.

Refinery
An industrial site where substances such as oil or sugar are cleaned and processed.

Renewable
Able to be used indefinitely because the supply will never run out.

Rig
Structure used for drilling for oil and gas.

Silt
Fine mud or clay at the bottom of a river or lake.

Slick
A thin layer of oil floating on water.

Smog
A polluting mixture of fog and smoke.

Solar power
Energy from sunlight.

Starch
A substance manufactured by plants that forms an important part of animal diets.

Turbines
Motors that are made to work by the power of wind, water or steam.

Uranium
A radioactive metallic element which is used as a fuel in nuclear power stations.

Further information

Books

World Energy Issues
Jim Pipe, Franklin Watts, 2010

Energy Now and In the Future series
Neil Morris, Franklin Watts, 2009

Using Energy (GreenTeam)
Sally Hewitt, Franklin Watts, 2008

Action for the Environment (Energy Supplies)
Chris Oxlade, Franklin Watts, 2004

Websites

www.eia.doe.gov/kids/
A great website with good information on all sources of energy plus games, puzzles and quizzes.

www.repp.org
Website for the Centre for Renewable Energy and Sustainable Technology.

www.direct.gov.uk/actonco2
Measure your carbon footprint and make your home more energy efficient.

www.paceproject.net
The Pan African Conservation Education Project exists to help spread simple solutions to environmental problems.

Index